Nicodemus
National Historic Site

In northwestern Kansas is a town that stands for freedom, opportunity, and family. It is a special place where roots run deep and every building has a story connecting family and friends. Year after year, people return to remember pioneering ancestors and to reacquaint themselves with friends and family who have moved away.

Located just off Highway 24 in Graham County today the town of Nicodemus is a small cluster of peaceful historic buildings, across the road from wheat fields that stretch to the northern horizon.

But in 1877 Nicodemus was the Promised Land to African Americans who were determined to make the most of new opportunities after the Civil War ended. With courage and perseverance but few material possessions, they made a new life for themselves in a challenging geographical setting.

Why Kansas?

With racial oppression rising after the Civil War in the waning days of Reconstruction, southern blacks began to look beyond the South for a better life. African Americans felt welcome in Kansas because so many of its citizens had paid such a bloody price in fighting pro-slavery Missourians before the Civil War so that Kansas could enter the Union a free state. To people denied property ownership, free land offered under the Homestead Act in Kansas and other western states was an irresistible lure.

The Promised Land

Before European settlement, semi-nomadic tribes of the Plains made temporary settlements in the area around what is now Nicodemus. They lived along the south fork of the Solomon River, where they built earthlodges, hunted wild game, and fished. They also gathered wild foods and grew corn, beans, and squash along the tree-lined banks of the Solomon River.

The landscape nearby was markedly different from these lush bottomlands. With an arid climate and sandy soil, most of the almost treeless land was virgin prairie. "The valley of the south fork of the Solomon is not, beyond Stockton, the most fertile or beautiful body of land on earth," wrote Clayton Fraser, a visitor to Nicodemus in 1881. "There is a proneness to sand; a tendency to cactus; a predilection in favor of soap weed. The 'magnesia,' as it is called, a sort of a compromise between a clay bank and a stone quarry, is quite apparent in the low bluffs."

What drew pioneers to this place?

As Nicodemus settler H. L. Vanderwall wrote in the *Cleveland Gazette* in 1884, "About six years ago we saw that the day for a black man to get property in the South was at an end and Ku-Klux rule commenced." By the late 1870s, the U.S. Army had surveyed Kansas and opened it for settlement. Investors and land speculators saw the opportunity to profit from this newly surveyed land in western Kansas.

In 1877, one week prior to the formal end of Reconstruction, six black men and one white man registered the Nicodemus Town Company with the Kansas Secretary of State for the purpose of developing and selling lots within the proposed town of Nicodemus. Reverend W. H. Smith was originally from Tennessee. Ben Carr, S. P. Roundtree, Jerry Allsap, Jeff Lenze, and William Edmonds came to Kansas from Kentucky. W. R. Hill, the lone white man, was originally from Indiana.

They chose a name for their settlement sure to resonate with the black farmers they hoped to enlist—Nicodemus. The mythical Nicodemus had been described as a "slave of African birth" who struggled for freedom and hoped for "the good time coming," according to one popular Civil War-era song, "Wake Nicodemus!"

On April 16, 1877, the first handbill advertising Nicodemus appeared. A leaflet undated (but known to be printed before May 15, 1877) entitled "The Largest Colored Colony in America!" said that by September 1, the colony would have houses erected and mercantile business opened for settlers. In addition to the handbills, several promoters traveled to the Lexington and Georgetown areas of Kentucky, speaking at local churches and enticing emigrants to Nicodemus with glowing descriptions of the rich soil, wild horses that could be tamed for farm work, and the abundance of wild game and timber.

By July 30, thirty new settlers, most from Topeka, and some of the town's officers arrived on the site. On September 17, 1877, the first formal group of 350 emigrants led by W. R. Hill arrived in Nicodemus from Fayette, Scott, and Bourbon Counties, Kentucky. What these new arrivals saw when they arrived at Nicodemus was much different than what they were led to expect.

First Impressions

Willina Hickman, a member of the first group to arrive in July, recalled her disappointment, "I looked with all the eyes I had. 'Where is Nicodemus? I don't see it.' My husband pointed out various smokes coming out of the ground and said, 'That is Nicodemus.' The families lived in dugouts… The scenery was not at all inviting, and I began to cry."

Not all of the original settlers' stories tell of heartache and tears. The story of Charles Williams and his wife Emma has endured through the generations and is still told today as an example of new beginnings at Nicodemus. The couple left the lush, rolling bluegrass of Kentucky with Emma pregnant with her first child. After a long trip westward and then a train from St. Louis to Ellis, Kansas, they disembarked in September 1877. From there, they trudged more than 30 miles northward to the treeless prairie of Nicodemus. They lived in a dugout during the bitterly cold Christmas holidays and the mild winter that followed. Henry Williams—the first child born in Nicodemus— began their family.

With grit and determination, newcomers to Nicodemus dug out homes in the bluffs of the Solomon River or hillsides. With only a few belongings and basic tools, they gradually made a life for themselves. Some sold buffalo bones for six dollars a ton to survive the first years. Others worked on the railroad and farmed on the side. Some industrious residents broke up their first acres of tough prairie sod with only the most minimal of garden implements—hoes, mattocks, and spades.

Because the land was almost treeless, Nicodemus residents cooked and heated their dugouts or sod homes with dried cow or buffalo chips, corn cobs, wood salvaged from the Solomon River, and sunflower stalks.

In 1877, the enterprising Zach T. Fletcher opened a general store and later a post office, both housed in his dugout. His wife taught school between 1879 and 1887 in various dugouts and sod houses. The first hotel, operated by A. T. Hall and E. P. McCabe, started off as a dugout before two sod hotels, Myers House and Union House, were built in 1879. Three of Nicodemus' first churches—two Baptist and one African Methodist Episcopal—held services in enlarged dugouts until the congregations could build sod structures.

Sod construction continued on into the early twentieth century. In 1902, Bernice A. Bates was born in a two-room sod house— "one to cook in, the other to sleep in," she recalled. She and her family lived there until 1911 when her father built a two-story frame house. Both dugouts and sod homes continued to exist in Nicodemus through the 1940s.

NICODEMUS.

Nicodemus was a slave of African birth,
  And was bought for a bag full of gold;
He was reckoned a part of the salt of the earth,
  But he died years ago, very old.

Nicodemus was a prophet, at least he was as wise,
  For he told of the battles to come ;
How we trembled with fear, when he rolled up his eyes,
  And we heeded the shake of his thumb.

CHORUS :   Good time coming, good time coming,
  Long, long time on the way ;
Run and tell Elija to hurry up Pomp,
  To meet us under the cottonwood tree,
In the Great Solomon Valley
  At the first break of day.

TOP: Lyrics to Civil-War era song
MIDDLE: First Baptist Church
BOTTOM: Re-enactors from the Nicodemus Buffalo Soldiers Association (10th Cavalry) attend the annual Homecoming celebration.

Social Activities in Nicodemus

In addition to the hard work of farming, residents made time for more social activities too. In early 1887, Nicodemus formed its first baseball team and, according to the custom at the time, named the team after the local newspaper. The Western Cyclone Baseball Club had a uniform of a black cap, white shirt with "Cyclone" written across the front, blue pants, red belt, and black stockings. The first game was with the "Prairie Muffers" of Sugar Loaf in nearby Rooks Country on 2 April 1887; the winner of that game is lost to time.

ABOVE: Nicodemus baseball team, 1907
OPPOSITE: Nicodemus residents gather in front of the William's store in the 1890s.

Simon P. Roundtree, a more prosperous resident, built the first stone house in Nicodemus in June of 1877. John Anderson built the second stone house in September 1877. The next year, Zach T. Fletcher moved out of his dugout and built a limestone structure as both a residence and place of business where he operated his St. Francis Hotel, a stagecoach station, and a post office. The St. Francis Hotel/Fletcher-Switzer Residence is one of the few early structures remaining in Nicodemus, and it is now a private residence.

By the spring of 1879, Nicodemus was comprised of thirty-five homes, a livery stable, two churches, a general store, post office, hotel, real estate office, and two schoolrooms. Farmers were able to purchase or borrow agricultural equipment in nearby Hill City to plow their fields. In 1887 the editor of the town's newspaper the *Western Cyclone* noted that "quite a lot of garden stuff comes into town [from farms.]"

By mid-1886, Nicodemus had fifteen stone buildings, fourteen farm buildings, seven sod structures, two churches, two hotels, two stables, one newspaper, one schoolroom, one land company, one bank, one society hall, and one hundred and fifty permanent residents. The next year, the town residents built their first formal schoolhouse, a two-story four-room frame structure located near the center of town.

The rapid development of Nicodemus in the late 1880s continued as two coal yards came to town in 1887, in preparation for what residents hoped would be the most exciting expansion yet—the railroad.

But the promised railway never materialized; the Union Pacific bypassed Nicodemus by six miles despite the town's lobbying. Drought, grasshopper plagues, and hard times followed. Residents took wage-paying jobs in towns. Many moved away to nearby Bogue, which had a railroad depot, or further west. Once-bustling Nicodemus became a rural farm town.

In 1907, the First Baptist Church was rebuilt of local limestone, now covered in stucco. The present Nicodemus School District No. 1 Building was constructed in 1918, following a fire that destroyed the original building. The school closed in 1955 and was later purchased by the American Legion for meetings and gatherings.

The Switzer family moved into what had been the St. Francis Hotel, originally a two-story structure with two rooms upstairs and two rooms downstairs. "When we got it," lifelong Nicodemus resident Ora Switzer recalled, "we had so many kids, we added on rooms, and bought houses and... had them moved in there. We fixed it up to suit ourselves." Today the building is known as the Fletcher-Switzer House.

Township Hall was built as a Work Projects Administration project in 1939 during the devastating dust bowl years. The hall and adjacent Township Park, constructed in 1982, have become community and tourist centers, as well as the central meeting place during the Emancipation Days Celebration, now called Nicodemus Homecoming.